NEW HORIZONS

science 5~16

KEY STAGE 2
Our living surroundings

Jacqueline Dineen

CAMBRIDGE
UNIVERSITY PRESS

Published by the Press Syndicate of the
University of Cambridge
The Pitt Building, Trumpington Street,
Cambridge CB2 1RP
10 West 20th Street, New York,
NY 10011-4211, USA
10 Stamford Road, Oakleigh,
Melbourne 3166, Australia

© Cambridge University Press 1993

First published 1993

Designed by Guy Hooper and Pardoe Blacker
Publishing Ltd, Shawlands Court,
Newchapel Road, Lingfield, Surrey RH7 6BL
Illustrated by Annabelle Brend, Dawn Brend,
Neil Bulpitt, Charlotte Cruise, Chris Forsey,
John Fox, Jenny Mumford, Greg Stewart

Printed in Great Britain at the University Press,
Cambridge

A catalogue record for this book is
available from the British Library

ISBN 0 521 39757 X

Photographic credits

t=top b=bottom c=centre l=left r=right

Cover: NHPA

5t Gérard Lacz/NHPA; 5b Brian Hawkes/NHPA; 6 John
Jeffrey/NHPA; 7b John Waters & Bernadette
Spiegel/Planet Earth Pictures; 10l, 10r, 11l, 11r
M. Nimmo/FLPA; 14t Ivan Polunin/NHPA; 15t Stephen
Dalton/NHPA; 16l John Shaw/NHPA; 17r Mary Evans
Picture Library; 18t Hans Reinhard/Bruce Coleman
Ltd; 19t Stephen Dalton/NHPA; 20c Laurie Campbell/
NHPA; 21t M. W. F. Tweedie/NHPA; 21b G. I. Bernard/
NHPA; 23t Morten Strange/NHPA; 23b M. Savonius/
NHPA; 26 Roger Wilmshurst/FLPA; 26 inset Alan
Williams/NHPA; 28b Stephen Dalton/ NHPA; 29t Bryan
& Cherry Alexander/NHPA; 31c Stephen Krasemann/
NHPA; 32t John Lythgoe/ Planet Earth Pictures;
33t Peter Johnson/NHPA; 34, 35 inset Jonathan Scott/
Planet Earth Pictures; 36c, 37t Martin Wendler/NHPA;
40c A. N. T/NHPA; 41t Anthony Bannister/NHPA;
43t Eric Soder/NHPA; 43b Michael Leach/NHPA ;
44b John Shaw/NHPA; 45c L. Lee Rue/FLPA;
46t Haraldo Palo/NHPA; 47r, 49c A. N. T/NHPA;
51t Jany Sauvanet/NHPA; 52b Herwarth Voigtmann/
Planet Earth Pictures; 53t A. N. T/NHPA; 54t Stephen
Dalton/NHPA; 55t David Curl/Oxford Scientific Films;
56t Nicholas de Vore/Bruce Coleman Ltd; 57t Bill
Leimbach/South American Pictures; 58l Ann Ronan
Picture Library; 58tr Geoff du Feu/Planet Earth
Pictures; 58br R. P. Lawrence/FLPA; 60b Greenpeace/
Colley; 60t Clem Haagner Okapia/ Oxford Scientific
Films; 61t John Shaw/NHPA; 61b David Woodfall/
NHPA.

Contents

Introduction

Living things can exist in almost every part of the world. In many cases, they can do this only because they have **adapted** or changed to suit the **environment** they live in.

In this book, we will study some of the world's environments and compare the animals and plants which live in them. Britain alone has several different environments, such as woodland, grassland, moorland, river, and coastline. Living things have adapted to different **climates** and surroundings.

Near the equator, the weather is hot and wet. Plants in the **tropical** rain forests grow big. Many different types of tree have developed in this climate. But the air is very **humid**. It is sticky and uncomfortable for animals that are not used to it.

In the savanna or grasslands of Africa, the climate is hot with a rainy season. The animals and plants here are different from those found in the **temperate** grasslands of Europe and North America.

Find out more about climates in the *New Horizons* book, *Life around us*.

4

The walrus

The Poles are at the furthest point north and furthest point south of the world. They are covered with ice and snow. Only a few types of plant can grow there. Some animals have managed to adapt to these conditions. Walruses live in the icy waters near the North Pole. They have developed long tusks which they use for digging shellfish off the sea bed. The walrus has a bag of skin on each side of its neck. These blow up and keep the walrus afloat when it is sleeping in the sea.

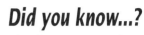

Did you know...?

The largest member of the walrus and seal family is the Southern elephant seal which lives near the South Pole. An average male is 5 m long and weighs 2270 kg.

Think of six wild animals that live in Africa and six that live in Britain. How are they different? How are they the same? Why are most of the wild animals in Britain not very big today?

Some environments are so **hostile** that nothing can grow there. But even on a bare rock, there may be colonies of birds nesting.

5

More about: rain forest pp38-39   savanna pp34-35   woodland pp18-19

What is a habitat?

A habitat is the place where an animal or plant lives. On land, most animals need food, water and shelter. They must find or adapt to a habitat which gives them these things.

A habitat can be identified by plants that grow in it. Forests and woodlands have trees which provide food and shelter for animals. In **deciduous** woods, the soil is rich because fallen leaves rot down and improve it. The soil in **coniferous** woods is poor.

Plants need a suitable climate with some sunshine and rain. The type of soil is also important. Soil with a lot of lime in it is called **alkaline** soil. Soil with very little lime is **acidic**. Between these two types is **neutral** soil. Some plants can grow only in acidic soil, others need alkaline or neutral conditions.

You can find out how alkaline or acidic soil is by testing it with pH paper. Test some soil samples from different places. What do you notice about the plants that grow there?

The needles from conifers take a long time to rot so they do not nourish the soil. Water drains away because there is no rotting vegetation to act as a 'sponge' to hold moisture in the soil.

Downland has chalky (alkaline) soil. The grass is short and springy and there are few trees. Moorlands are bleak and windswept. The soil is acidic. Only heathers and coarse grasses can grow there.

All these habitats have animals which have adapted to the different surroundings. Moors support only small trees, so moorland birds build their nests on the ground. Rabbits live on open land as well as in woods. They provide their own shelter by digging burrows.

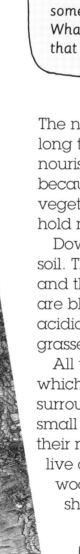

In which habitat does this great spotted woodpecker live?

pH testing of soil types

a lot of lime

not much lime

Can you identify these plants?

acidic soil

neutral soil

alkaline soil

Rivers, lakes and seas are also habitats. Life in the water is different from life on land, but animals still need to find food and escape from their enemies.

Wildlife corridors

Hedgerows were planted by farmers to enclose their fields, but they now form a wildlife habitat.

There are about 1 million km of hedgerows in Britain. More than 500 **species** of wild flowers have been found in them. These attract insects which are food for birds and small mammals. Animals move from place to place through the hedgerows, which give them shelter. That is why the hedgerows are called 'wildlife corridors'.

7

More about: downlands pp26-27 sea pp22-23, 46, 52-53

Developing and changing

The pronghorn antelope evolved in North America and is not found in any other part of the world. Other deer and antelope spread between North America and Europe.

Animals and plants have been developing and adapting for millions of years. This is called **evolution**. Living things evolve in the environment that suits them best.

Climates have also changed. Continents have broken up and moved apart. Many animals and plants adapted to these changes or moved to a different habitat.

Some animals could not adapt and so they became **extinct**. The dinosaurs were reptiles which died out 65 million years ago. This may have been because they could not adapt when the climate changed.

Where animals evolved

Animals could spread across the world if the climate is right and there is land to cross. Parts of Europe had a tropical climate 2 million years ago. Giraffes, elephants, hippopotamuses and apes lived there. These animals became extinct in the north during the ice ages.

North and South America were not joined together until 3 million years ago. But Alaska and Siberia were joined, so animals could make the journey between Eurasia and North America by that route.

The three-toed sloth developed in the trees of the South American forests. It is a forest animal so it did not spread to North America.

Find out more about dinosaurs in the *New Horizons* books, *Life around us* and *Land, water and air*.

Some animals are still found only in the place where they evolved.

Find out more about evolution and the changing continents in the *New Horizons* book, *Land, water and air*.

The desert dormouse is found only in Eurasia. Other rodents have spread all over the world.

Elephants evolved in Africa and gradually spread to other places.

Gibbons are found only in India and the Far East.

Find out more about fossils and the ice ages in the *New Horizons* book, *Land, water and air*.

The sea is another type of habitat. Life on Earth started in the water.

Australia became an isolated continent millions of years ago. It has its own wildlife, such as kangaroos and koala bears.

Did you know...?

The fossil remains of hippopotamuses and rhinoceroses have been found in the sands underneath Trafalgar Square in London.

9

More about: adapting pp4-5, 14-17 climate pp40, 44, forests pp38-43

How to study a habitat

Find out more about the seasons in the *New Horizons* book, *Life around us*.

You can find out how plants and animals make use of their surroundings by studying one habitat more closely.

In Britain and other temperate regions, there are four seasons. You need to study the habitat in each season to see how life changes.

Spring

Winter

What should you look for?

If you choose a land habitat, look at:

The landscape
- Is it flat or hilly?
- Are there trees?
- Is it sheltered from strong winds?
- How do the trees growing in a sheltered valley compare with trees or shrubs growing on a windswept hillside?

Soil
- Does it contain a lot of sand or clay or chalk?

The table below will help you to find out.

Soil type	What happens when wet?	What happens when dry?
sandy soil	lumpy but difficult to roll into a ball	falls apart
clay soil	very sticky holds together well	stays stuck in a ball
chalky soil	sticky and slippery	crumbly because water seeps out of it quickly

Flora and fauna

- Which plants grow in the habitat?
- Which minibeasts live in the soil?
- Which birds can you identify?
- Do any mammals live there?

You will need books about wildlife to help you identify the different species.

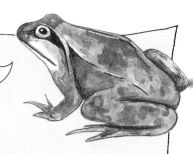

Find out more about rock pools and ponds as habitats in the *New Horizons* book, *Life around us*.

Summer

Keep a record of everything you can find out about the habitat, such as the type of landscape, the temperature at the surface of the soil, the date, the time, whether it is sunny or cloudy, and so on.

You can then make a study of another habitat. If the first was grassland, you might choose woodland. Or you could study a water habitat such as a pond or river. Compare the species you find. Which are different? Which are the same?

Autumn

Gardens have become new habitats for wildlife. Some mammals and birds have become urbanised and used to people. Look for evidence of this in the area where you live.

Watching wildlife

Many wild animals are shy and easily frightened. When you are watching them, keep well hidden. If you have to get closer, move slowly and quietly. Never pull up wild flowers or disturb birds' nests.

Sparrows are very widespread because they have adapted to several different habitats. Can you find other examples of animals which are common because they have adapted to different conditions?

You might decide to compare two watery habitats, such as a rock pool and a pond. What differences would you expect to find?

11

More about: habitats pp6-7 plants pp6-7, 12-13 soil pp6-7, 24, 26

Identifying plant groups

When you are studying a habitat, you may come across plants which you cannot find in your books. How do you identify them?

First, you have to decide which group the plant is in. All plants fit into one of five main groups. The most simple are mosses and liverworts. Then there are ferns, conifers, and flowering plants. The most simple flowering plants grow from bulbs, and have narrow pointed leaves with straight veins and parts of their flowers in threes. The most complicated are the flowering plants with two halves to their seeds, such as beans, peas and peanuts.

> Find out more about different types of plants in the *New Horizons* book, *Life around us.*

Using a key

When you have decided which group a plant fits into, you can start to find out exactly what it is. You can use a key to help you. You start by asking questions about the plant.

1 Do the flowers have round heads?
  Yes The plant could be daisy or thrift or clover or dandelion or thistle.
  No Go to 2.

daisy

2 Are the flowers in clusters?
  Yes The plant could be cow parsley or meadowsweet.
  No Go to 3.

cow parsley

3 Does the flower have petals of different sizes?
  Yes The plant could be violet or snowdrop or iris or orchid or larkspur.
  No Go to 4.

iris

When you know the answer to the first question, you can move on to the next question. Below is an example for a flowering plant. When you have worked through this key, ask questions about the leaves and stems.

4 Does the flower have four petals?

Yes The plant could be poppy or traveller's joy or a willow-herb or heather.

No Go to 5.

poppy

5 Does the flower have five petals?

Yes The plant could be herb-Robert or meadow crane's-bill or fairy flax or periwinkle or a gentian or pimpernel or rock-rose.

No Go to 6.

periwinkle

6A Is the flower bell-shaped?

The plant could be a bluebell.

6B Is the flower trumpet-shaped?

The plant could be a daffodil.

Did you know...?

- Scientists think there are more than 350 000 different species of plants in the world.

- Hawthorns, raspberries and mountain ash trees are all members of the rose family.

Make your own key for plants you know about. Then make a key for animals. Ask questions like: Has the animal got a backbone? Has the animal got feathers?

1. Does the animal have fur?

   Yes   Animal could be...

   No   Go to 2

2. Does the animal have scales?

   Yes   Animal could be...

   No   Go to 3

13

More about: conifers pp6, 42-43 habitats pp6-7, 10-11

Survival

Animals and plants must be well adapted and have the ability to change with environmental conditions in order to survive. They also have to compete for the things they need to live.

Some plants have become so good at competing that they can take over from other plants. A poppy plant produces about 20 000 seeds which can lie in the soil for many years. When the field is ploughed, the seeds come to the surface and start to grow very quickly. If the farmer lets them, the poppies will take over from the crops in the field.

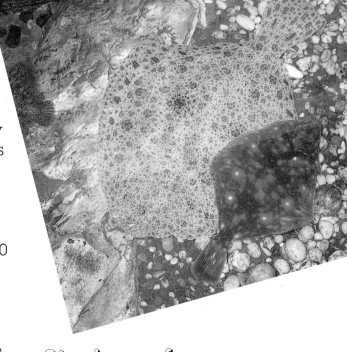

Herbivores eat plants. **Carnivores** eat meat. They hunt and eat the herbivores or other carnivores. The big wild cats of Africa are meat-eaters, so are foxes, and **domestic** cats and dogs.

Staying safe

Some herbivores have developed ways of escaping from **predators**. Zebras live in large herds because single animals are at far greater risk. In a herd, only one or two animals will be killed at a time. Gazelles escape by running very fast across the African plains.

Find out more about camouflage and danger signals in the *New Horizons* book, *Life around us.*

Some animals are camouflaged. Brill and plaice are fish which live on and in the sea bed. Their colour matches the sand, mud and stones of the sea bed. Can you think of any animals which change colour to camouflage themselves?

Fierce insects

Some insects are fierce predators. A tarantula spider, which can measure 25 cm across, hunts and kills birds, lizards and small rodents such as mice. The giant water bug catches tadpoles and small fish.

The praying mantis grabs frogs, lizards and butterflies with its strong front legs.

Insects can stay safe by using camouflage or by pretending to be something else. One type of Brazilian beetle can flatten itself so that it looks like a bird's dropping.

Some insects look like dead leaves. When danger threatens, they lie among real dead leaves.

Did you know...?

The North American skunk produces a foul-smelling liquid which puts off even the hungriest predator. Its black and white colouring acts as a warning to other animals.

15

More about: adapting pp4-5, 8-9 plants pp6-7, 12-13 predators p35

Adapting to surroundings

You can see how animals have adapted to almost every environment by comparing different species of the same animal.

Bears

Bears are found in Europe, Asia and North America. Northern bears such as the grizzly bear of North America have big, heavy bodies and thick, shaggy coats to protect them from the cold.

Polar bears have developed white coats so that they can blend into the snowy world of the North Pole. This is important because they are hunters and need to sneak up on their **prey**. Their partly-webbed feet help them to swim among the ice floes, catching fish.

Malaysian bears live in a tropical climate. They are small with thin black coats.

The snowshoe hare from Canada needs to save its body heat. It has short ears and legs.

The black-tailed jackrabbit lives in the southern USA. Its ears and legs are shorter than the antelope jackrabbit's.

Did you know...?

Kodiak bears live on Kodiak island off the coast of Alaska. It is so cold that the bears have grown into giants. They are nearly 3 m tall and weigh 760 kg.

The Arctic hare is white with very short ears and legs.

Rabbits and hares

Animals which live in hot climates need to shed body heat. Long ears and legs help them do this.

The antelope jackrabbit lives in Central America, where it is hot. It has very long ears and legs.

Britain has a large range of habitats and wildlife for such a small island. The next six spreads look at some of these.

Survival of the fittest

A scientist called Charles Darwin discovered that animals and plants have adapted and developed over millions of years. In 1831, Darwin was invited to go on an expedition to South America on *HMS Beagle*. On the Galapagos Islands near the equator, he found 13 types of finch. Each type had developed a differently-shaped beak to suit the food supply. Darwin came to the conclusion that animals and plants had to adapt to survive. Those that could not adapt died out.

17

More about: islands pp50-51 plants pp12-13 survival pp14-15

Deciduous woodlands

Britain has coniferous, mixed and deciduous woodlands. Coniferous trees have adapted to cold climates. They have narrow, waxy needles which do not lose much water. Deciduous woods change the most with the seasons because the trees lose their leaves in winter.

In autumn, the leaves turn red and brown and fall from the trees. The floor of the wood is carpeted in leaf litter. Insects burrow in the leaves and toadstools appear. The toadstools feed on the dead leaves and rotting wood.

In winter the trees are bare and the woods are quiet. There is not much food for the animals.

Great tits balance on the bare branches, searching for insects.

The wood at night

At night, the wood changes again. The daytime animals are asleep but foxes, hedgehogs and badgers come out to hunt for food. Owls swoop down on mice and voles. Many **nocturnal** animals have developed large eyes which can see in dim light. They can hunt for food without being seen. Many also have a keen sense of hearing. Others, like the bat, use their squeaking sound and large ears to pick up echoes, which tell them if there is an insect near for them to catch.

Hedgehogs and dormice have adapted to this shortage of food by hibernating. They can go without food because they do not need as much energy as when they are active.

Jays dig up their secret stores of acorns. Other animals store food in autumn to eat in winter. Grey squirrels hunt for the nuts they have buried.

Birds such as flycatchers and warblers return after migrating south to warmer countries for the winter.

In spring, buds appear on the trees. Once the trees are in leaf, there will be less sunlight for the plants on the woodland floor. Bluebells and primroses have adapted by flowering before the trees are in leaf.

In summer, everything is in full bloom and all the birds have returned.

Find out more about the seasons in the *New Horizons* book, *Life around us*.

Follow the animal tracks

When there is snow on the ground, you can see the tracks of animals and birds in the woods. If you can study a wood in winter, try to find out which tracks are which. You may see the tracks of rabbits, hares, foxes, badgers and squirrels, and the spiky prints of birds' feet. There may be holes in the snow where squirrels have been digging for nuts. Foxes also dig into the snow, hunting for small rodents. Can you identify these tracks?

More about: coniferous trees pp6, 42-43 survival pp14-15

Fields and hedgerows

Some fields are used for growing crops. Others are grassy meadows where animals graze.

Thousands of years ago, most of Britain was covered with dense woodlands. Grass grew only in small areas where there were no trees. As more and more trees were chopped down, grass began to take over.

Fields are usually private property, but there are sometimes public footpaths across them. Never trespass on to farmland and always shut gates behind you. Follow the Country Code.

In spring, wild flowers such as buttercups, daisies and red clover appear among the grass.

Many hedgerows are full of wild flowers, like primroses, red campion, bluebells and cow parsley. There are also climbers such as honeysuckle.

Bird's-foot trefoil, with its bright yellow flowers, is one of the most common grassland flowers.

Compare a field and a hedgerow at different seasons. What do you notice? Keep a record of everything you find out.

Find out more about fields and hedgerows in another *New Horizons* book, *Life around us.*

Did you know...?

- There are more than 150 species of wild grasses in Britain today.
- In late summer and autumn, you can sometimes see flocks of greenfinches, goldfinches and linnets raiding the fields for spilt grain.

There may be butterflies such as the common blue (above) and the brimstone.

Some common birds of the fields and hedgerows are yellowhammers, corn buntings and partridges.

Ploughing time

In autumn, the crops have been harvested and the farmer ploughs the fields. As the plough turns the earth, hordes of minibeasts come to the surface. There are earthworms, leatherjackets, beetles and millipedes. Flocks of gulls, jackdaws and other birds follow the plough, feasting on these **invertebrates** before they have time to burrow into the earth again.

Small animals, such as mice, voles, grasshoppers, earthworms, ladybirds, beetles and bees live in the grass.

More about: flowers pp12-13 grassland pp26-27, 34-37

By the sea

Britain has a long coastline made up of steep cliffs, sand and shingle beaches, flat marshes and estuaries. Seaside plants have to cope with strong winds and salty air. There are few trees. In spring and summer, you can see brightly coloured flowers such as thrift bloom among the coarse grass on the cliffs.

The life of a sand dune

Sand dunes form in places where the wind and sea carry the sand inland. At first, the sand is blown about every time there is a strong wind.

Sand does not hold water, so plants which grow in this habitat have adapted so that they do not lose water easily. Plants lose water through their leaves. Marram grass has leaves which are rolled inwards to cut down on water loss. Sea holly and other plants have tough, waxy leaves.

As the dune builds up, the sand is deep enough for brambles and small shrubs to grow. Wildfowl nest in wet areas, called 'slacks' and 'lows', where pools of water collect.

A river estuary

Where rivers flow into the sea, there are estuaries with mudflats and salt marshes. As the tide goes out, thousands of cockles, mussels, ragworms, lugworms and tiny snails are left in the mud. In winter, huge flocks of oyster catchers, curlews and godwits fly in to feed in the mud on the water's edge. In spring, they are joined by birds migrating from Africa to the Arctic who stop for a

Gulls and terns are two seabirds which live in all coastal habitats. Can you find out about any others?

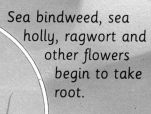

Marram grass is one of the first plants to grow on the dunes. Its long roots hold the sand together.

Sea bindweed, sea holly, ragwort and other flowers begin to take root.

Building a salt marsh

As a river flows into the sea, it drops mud and silt at its mouth. Gradually, this builds up into mudflats and salt marshes. Plants soon **colonise** the new land. In summer, salt marshes are full of sea lavender and sea aster. Above the tide level, grass begins to grow.

meal at the estuary. In autumn, these birds stop again on their way back to warmer lands.

Did you know...?

On some estuaries there are 50 000 small animals per square metre of mud.

In some places, rough seas have hurled shingle into ridges. Sea kale (above), yellow horned poppies and dock grow on shingle ridges.

23

More about: flowers pp12-13, 20 leaves pp6, 32-33 sea pp52-53

Heaths and moorlands

About 5000 years ago, during the New Stone Age, early farmers began to chop and burn down forests so that they could grow crops on the land. When the land had no more **nutrients** left in it, the people moved on and cleared another section of forest.

The cleared land was ruined. There were no tree roots to hold the soil together. Burning destroyed the plant material which gave the soil its nutrients. Rain washed away the minerals, so the soil became acidic.

Few trees could grow on this poor soil. But plants of one sort or another will take over most areas of land.

Merlins, hobbies and peregrine falcons circle above, watching for prey.

More rain fell on higher ground. The soil was peaty with less sand than the heaths, so it held water more easily. These areas became bleak moorland where only **hardy** plants like heather can survive.

The soil of the lowland areas was dry and sandy. These areas became heaths covered with gorse, coarse grasses and heather.

Grouse nest in the moorland heather and feed on heather shoots.

Some of Britain's reptiles, such as adders and sand lizards, **thrive** in the dry warmth of sandy heathland.

24

Night on the heath

Heaths and moors are wild places, particularly at night. Nocturnal animals come out in search of food. Mice hunt for food in heather and bracken. Owls fly silently through the air, waiting to pounce. As soon as dusk falls, nightjars leave their ground nests to hunt for moths.

Did you know...?

The tiger beetle has huge jaws. It flies very fast over the heath, chasing insects.

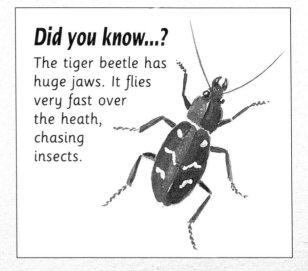

Animals and insects have adapted to live on heaths and moorlands. Sheep can survive on coarse grass and their thick, woolly coats protect them from harsh weather.

Food is scarce and so some of the insects have become predators. There are dragonflies, flying beetles, ants and hunting wasps.

Birds of heaths and moors nest on the ground. Stone curlews nest in the rough grass of heathlands.

Very waterlogged areas where rain collected turned into peat bogs where bog mosses and cotton grass grow.

25

More about: forests pp40-43   nocturnal animals pp54-55

Downlands

The Downs of southern England are ranges of chalk and limestone hills. They are not bleak like the moors, but they can be windswept. Not many trees grow there. Hardy trees and shrubs like hawthorn are often twisted into strange shapes by the wind.

The song of the skylark can be heard high above the Downs in spring and summer. On the ground, the loudest sound is the chirrup of grasshoppers.

For centuries, shepherds grazed their sheep on the Downs. The sheep cropped the springy turf short. Only small, slow-growing plants could survive the sheep's nibbling, and the alkaline soil.

In spring and early summer, the Downs are colourful with cowslips, harebells, violets and orchids. You can smell the scent of wild thyme and other herbs.

The wild flowers on the downlands provide food for many insects, particularly butterflies. The most common are the meadow brown, and the family of blue butterflies which includes the common blue and the chalkhill blue.

Today, few people live on the Downs because of the steep landscape and also because there are no rivers and streams to provide water. In some places, farmers have built dewponds to collect dew for animals to drink. Ancient footpaths across the downlands are still used by walkers. These paths link Iron Age hill forts.

Find out more about dewponds in another *New Horizons* book, *Land, water and air.*

Today, many farmers have turned to crop farming and so there are fewer sheep on the Downs.

Rabbits still keep the grass short, but in some places tangled, shrubby woodland is returning.

Did you know...?

Small cushion-like hillocks on the Downs are the homes of yellow field ants. About 25 000 ants live in the chambers and passages under each mound. People think that some of these mounds are 150 years old.

27

More about: butterflies p21   rabbits pp16-17   sheep p25

A river

The animals and plants found in a river change as the river flows to the sea. The river is divided into **reaches**.

In the upper reach, a small stream rushes down a hill or mountainside. In the middle reach, the river is wider and flows more slowly.

In the lower reach, the river winds slowly through a flat plain to the sea. Salt water may be forced up the river as the tide comes in.

The upper reach

Not many species of wildlife have adapted to the fast-flowing water here.

A dipper searches for insect larvae. It can walk under the water along the river bed, looking for food.

Sticklebacks are the smallest freshwater fish.

Moss and algae cling to the stones. They hide the larvae of insects such as the caddisfly and the stonefly. Insect larvae are food for the trout, the grayling, the stone loach and other fish of the upper reach.

Water voles tunnel into the river bank to make their homes.

Some caddisfly larvae surround themselves with a case made of twigs and sand. This protects them from predators and the fast-flowing river.

The yellow flag, or wild iris, flowers from May to July.

roach

freshwater shrimps

perch

pike

clams

Salmon lay their eggs in the upper reaches of a river. When the young fish hatch, they swim out to sea. They stay there until they are ready to lay their eggs and mate. Then they swim from the sea back to the upper reaches of the river they were born in.

If we study habitats in different parts of the world, we can see how living things have adapted to different climates and conditions...

water weeds and sedges

The middle reach

More, different species can survive in the slower waters of the middle reach. Barbels hide under weeds on the river bed and feed on mayfly larvae, snails and water plants. Dace live in shoals near the surface.

The lower reach

The largest variety of wildlife is found here.

Sea fish such as flounder and mullet come in with the tide.

Herons and kingfishers catch fish in the lower reach.

eels

29

More about: predators pp14-15   sea pp22-23, 52-53

In the desert

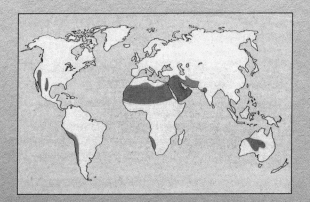

The desert is one of the most difficult environments for animals and plants to live in. The sun shines down all day from a cloudless sky. There are few plants to provide any shade. It is so hot that most animals hide in burrows or under stones during the day.

At night, the temperature falls to freezing point because there are no clouds to act as a blanket and trap heat. Animals must come out and hunt for food before it gets too cold.

Desert look-alikes

Animals which live in deserts on different continents have adapted in similar ways. This is called **convergent evolution**. The kangaroo rat of the North American desert looks similar to the African jerboa. It has long hind legs so that it can bound away from predators. The kit fox of North America is similar to the fennec. It has large ears which help it to hear prey and also to shed body heat.

The desert comes to life as soon as the sun goes down. The Sahara in Africa is the largest desert in the world.

As soon as it is dark, jerboas and ground squirrels hop out to find food from the few plants.

They will also eat locusts.

Reptiles in the desert

Reptiles such as lizards and snakes cannot control the temperature of their bodies. They need sunshine to warm their bodies but they must not get too hot or too cold. The desert lizard comes out of its burrow in the early morning to bask in the sun and hunt for prey. At midday it hides from the sun and comes out again in the afternoon. It warms its body up thoroughly before going back to its burrow for the night.

The Gila monster (below), found in the deserts of south-western USA and Mexico, and the Mexican beaded lizard are the only two **venomous** lizards in the world. They are covered with black, red, orange or yellow bead-like scales. These lizards eat insects, birds' eggs, young birds and even a nestful of mice. The Gila monster grows to about 50 cm long. The Mexican beaded lizard can grow to 90 cm!

Did you know...?

The Kalahari ground squirrel is one animal which can stay out in the midday sun. It uses its bushy tail as a shady parasol.

Fennec foxes are on the trail of the jerboas and ground squirrels.

Their large ears pick up the slightest sound in the dark.

31

More about: plants pp12-13 predators pp14-15

The search for water

If you were stuck in the desert without any water, you would die in a day or two. But desert animals and plants have adapted in several ways.

An oasis is a place in the desert where underground water comes to the surface. Date palms and other crops can grow round an oasis and animals go there to drink.

boojum tree

The African baobab and the Californian boojum tree have swollen trunks where water is stored.

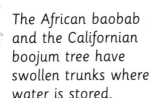

gum cistus

Some plants, such as gourds, have long roots to reach water far below the surface.

Plants with large leaves could not survive because water evaporates out of the leaves. Desert plants have small leaves or spines.

cactus

Water on the wing

Birds have to find water for themselves and their chicks. The sand grouse nests in the African desert. The male flies to a water hole and drinks. Then he soaks his breast feathers, which are specially designed to absorb water. He flies back to the nest and the chicks suck water from his feathers.

There is enough moisture in seeds for the kangaroo rat. But larger mammals have to make sure they are somewhere near a water hole for a daily drink.

Some animals can survive with very little water. Some animals never drink at all. The fennec fox and the jackal can get enough liquid from the bodies of the animals they kill.

Did you know...?

The driest place in the world is the Atacama Desert in Chile, South America. In 1971, it rained for the first time in 400 years.

The camel and the cactus

The camel does not store water in its hump, as many people think. The camel stores body fat there. When food and water are scarce, the camel uses this fat for energy. Fat can also be broken down to form water. When a camel does find water, it can drink 135 litres in 15 minutes.

Cacti are plants which grow naturally in the dry regions of North, Central and South America only. They have spines instead of broad leaves so that they do not lose water by evaporation. The cactus stem stores as much water as possible during the rains. The stored water makes the stem swell.

33

More about: birds pp24-26, 29, 36, 39, 51 leaves p6

The African savanna

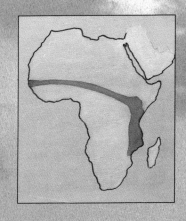

The savanna is a huge open expanse of tropical grassland in East Africa. There is a dry season and a wet season. During the dry season, the grass is yellow and parched. When the rains come, it soon turns green and flowers bloom.

Some grasses are 1 m high. There are few trees because the climate is dry for long parts of the year. The baobab and acacia are two common trees of the savanna. The acacia has small leaves which drop off when there is not enough water. They grow again after the rains.

Animals of the savanna

There is enough food to support many big mammals. The tallest animal is the giraffe which feeds on acacia leaves. It can reach leaves as high as 6 m above the ground. Other giants of the savanna are the rhinoceros and the elephant. Elephants need a quarter of a tonne of food a day and this means uprooting whole trees and pulling up mounds of grass. But this is not as destructive as it sounds. It lets light into the tangled grass and bushes, so that more plants can grow.

Did you know...?

There are more than 70 different kinds of antelope in Africa. The smallest is the dik-dik of the savanna. It is only 35 cm tall and has to leap high above the long grass to see what is happening.

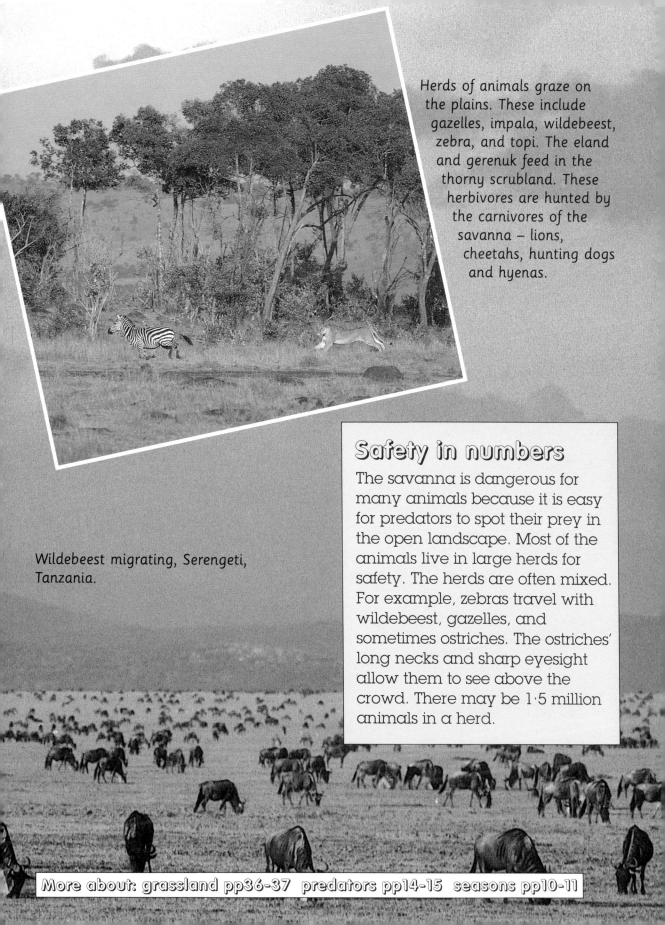

Herds of animals graze on the plains. These include gazelles, impala, wildebeest, zebra, and topi. The eland and gerenuk feed in the thorny scrubland. These herbivores are hunted by the carnivores of the savanna – lions, cheetahs, hunting dogs and hyenas.

Wildebeest migrating, Serengeti, Tanzania.

Safety in numbers

The savanna is dangerous for many animals because it is easy for predators to spot their prey in the open landscape. Most of the animals live in large herds for safety. The herds are often mixed. For example, zebras travel with wildebeest, gazelles, and sometimes ostriches. The ostriches' long necks and sharp eyesight allow them to see above the crowd. There may be 1·5 million animals in a herd.

More about: grassland pp36-37   predators pp14-15   seasons pp10-11

The pampas of South America

The pampas are grasslands south of the tropics in South America. Near the Atlantic Ocean, there is plenty of rain and the rich grass makes good grazing for Argentina's beef cattle. The western pampas are dry.

Animals of the pampas

There are no giant mammals or herds of grazing antelope on the pampas. Most of the grass-eaters are rodents. Cavies, or wild guinea pigs, tunnel through the grass.

The mara is a larger type of cavy which lives in a burrow. The behaviour of maras is similar to antelope in many ways. They live in herds and can run at up to 30 km/h on their long legs.

The largest animal on the pampas is the rhea, a flightless bird. It will eat insects and small rodents, but its main food is grass.

Predators and prey

The grass-eaters have the same problem as those on the savanna. They are easy to see on the open pampas, and predators are waiting to pounce. The pampas fox and the maned wolf prowl the pampas, hunting for cavies and smaller prey such as young birds and lizards. Hawks wait to swoop on cavies. The grass-eaters have adapted to protect themselves. They can all run fast or burrow into the ground when danger threatens.

The largest rodent

Farther north, near the Orinoco River in Venezuela, are another type of grasslands called llanos. For part of the year, the llanos are flooded by torrential rain. The animals of the llanos have adapted to living in water during the floods. The capybara is a giant guinea pig which is the size of a pig. It can live on dry land but when the floods come, it takes to the water and feeds on the sodden grass under the surface. Its eyes, ears and nose are on the top of its head and it has webbed feet to help it swim.

Did you know...?

One of the strangest animals on the pampas is the giant anteater. It has a long thin head which it pokes into ants' and termites' nests. Its sticky tongue is 60 cm long and comes out coated with insects. The giant anteater can eat about 30 000 ants and termites in a day.

37

More about: antelope p35 grasslands pp20-21, 34-35 predators pp14-15

Rain forests

In the tropics near the equator, the weather is the same all the year round. It is always hot and a lot of rain falls. These conditions are ideal for plants. They grow fast and form forests of huge trees.

The forest is so dense that hardly any light gets through to the forest floor. Climbing plants called lianas twine themselves between the trees. High up in the tree-tops, there is plenty of light and food. This is where most of the animals live. The rain forests of South America, Africa and Asia each have their own species of wildlife which are not found elsewhere.

The crowns of the trees touch each other and form a ceiling across the forest.

Monkeys and birds such as toucans and parrots feed on fruit from the trees.

Flying snakes can glide from one tree to another.

On the ground a few shrubs manage to grow in the dark forest. Few animals live here.

There are insects such as termites and ants.

Arrow poison frogs fight for territory.

The South American rain forest

The emergent level is formed by a few giant trees that have pushed their way above the rest. The silk cotton tree can grow to 70 m tall.

The fierce giant eagle, the harpy, nests here. It watches from its tree-top perch, then plunges through the trees to catch monkeys and birds.

The canopy is where most of the animals live.

Hummingbirds and butterflies take nectar from the brightly-coloured flowers in the trees.

Did you know...?

- There are more than 1600 species of birds in the Amazon rain forest.
- South American monkeys can grip with their tails as well as with their hands and feet.

The sloth moves extremely slowly along the branches, eating leaves.

The ocelot and margay are tree cats. They wait to pounce on monkeys.

The tamandua is an anteater which feeds on termites.

The Brazilian tapir feeds on the sparse leaves of the undergrowth.

39

More about: anteaters p37 forests pp40-43

Tropical seasonal forests

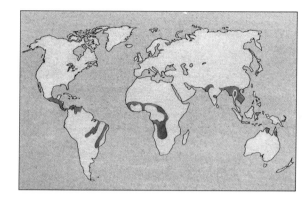

On the borders of the rain forests the weather is warm all year round, but there is a wet season and a dry season. It is not as dry as the savanna. There is enough rain for trees to grow, but there are also periods of **drought**.

The forests in these regions are called tropical seasonal forests. Plants have adapted to cope with months of dry weather.

Monsoon

The length of the dry season varies from place to place, but it always lasts several months. In India and South East Asia, the rainy season is called the **monsoon**. Heavy rain falls during the summer months and it is dry from November to April.

There are tropical seasonal forests in northern India, South East Asia, South America, Africa, and northern Australia.

Find out more about monsoons in the *New Horizons* book, *Land, water and air*.

Trees grow close together forming a **canopy** where animals live. The Indian banyan and the Australian eucalyptus have tough evergreen leaves which can survive long dry spells. Teak and mountain ebony are tropical deciduous trees. They lose their leaves during the dry season.

Fruit-eaters

In the monsoon forests of northern India, fruit bats, langur monkeys and hornbills feed on fruit. Hornbills pull a fruit off the tree with their long beaks. Then they throw the fruit in the air, catch it and swallow it. Fruit-eaters help to spread the seeds of plants. The animal eats the whole fruit, seeds and all. The seeds pass right through its body and come out in its droppings, some distance from the original tree.

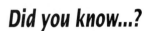

Did you know...?

- The jungle fowl, which is found in South East Asia, is the ancestor of the domesticated chicken.

- The fruit bat comes out to feed at night. It cannot perch on a branch like a bird. It has to grab fruit in its mouth as it flies by.

okapi

Animals of the forest floor

On the ground, Indian elephants browse among the trees, unlike the African elephant which lives on the plains. The okapi, a type of giraffe, also lives on the forest floor. The guinea fowl and the cassowary are two birds which live on the ground.

41

More about: elephants pp9, 34, 58 forests pp38-39, 42-43

Northern coniferous forests

The northern forests stretch in a belt right round the top of the world, across North America, Europe and Russia. The summers are hot, but the winters are long and bitterly cold so plants have to be hardy to survive.

Trees of the forest

The forests are very dark because the trees grow close together. Most of the trees are conifers which have adapted to survive in cold, dry climates. They include spruce, fir, pine and larch. The giant redwoods of North America tower over other trees. There may be a few hardy deciduous trees such as birch and willow.

The forest floor is covered with a thick carpet of fallen needles, which take a long time to rot. Few other plants can grow in these conditions.

Reindeer, roe deer, caribou and moose strip the bark from the trees or eat mosses and lichens that grow on them.

Finding food

Food is **scarce**, particularly in winter. Insects and a few birds, including the capercaillie and the pine grosbeak, feed on the needles from the trees. Other birds are insect-eaters. The caterpillars of the pine beauty moth eat pine needles. The crested tit reaches into the needles with its thin beak to find the caterpillars.

The seeds in the cones provide food for birds, squirrels, voles and other small mammals.

The lynx (above), weasel, pine marten, wild cat and wolf are all meat-eaters of the forest. They often hunt animals far larger than themselves. A weasel will kill a rabbit. A lynx hunts deer.

Did you know...?

Conifers are shaped like cones, with branches that slope downwards. A heavy covering of winter snow can slide off without breaking the branches.

The crossbill is a type of finch which has a specially-adapted beak with crossed tips. It uses its beak to force the scales of a cone open and takes out each seed with its tongue.

43

More about: conifers pp6, 18   deciduous trees pp6, 18-19   forests pp38-41

The tundra

To the south of the North Pole, where the ice cap ends, there is a cold desert called the tundra. It is dark for several months during the winter and the temperature is well below freezing.

In the summer

The summer lasts for three or four months only. Even then, it is often freezing, but the days are very long. There is enough sunshine for plants to grow, though there are no tall trees.

Did you know...?

The Arctic is a land-locked sea at the North Pole. There are many large land animals living at the Arctic Circle which have reached it from North America, Greenland, Europe and Asia.

At the first sign of sunshine, dwarf shrubs and clumps of plants burst into bloom, making the most of the sunshine before they are plunged into darkness again.

The sun melts frost on the surface but underneath, the soil remains solid and is called **permafrost**.

Plants cannot put down long roots. The only trees are dwarf willow and dwarf birch, which are a few centimetres high. There are tussocks of coarse grass.

The animals of the tundra

Polar bears and musk oxen live in the tundra all year round. Polar bears are meat-eaters in the water, but they eat plants on land where meat is scarce. Lemmings live under the snow, feeding on plants. They are prey for the meat-eaters, such as the ermine and the Arctic fox.

In summer, more animals arrive to make the most of the new plants and the millions of insects which have hatched out. Ducks fly in to feed on water plants in the lakes. Turnstones and other birds feed on insects, and the lemmings are food for birds of prey such as snowy owls and ravens.

Each summer, large herds of caribou journey up from the coniferous forests in Canada. They spread out on the tundra, grazing on lichens. At the end of August, they gather into herds again and set off on the long trek back to Canada.

Find out more about migrating animals in the *New Horizons* book, *Life around us.*

All change

In winter, many of the tundra animals have white coats so that they merge into the snowy background. In summer, when the snow melts, Arctic foxes, Arctic hares and snowy owls shed their thick white coats to reveal brown ones which have been growing underneath.

45

More about: habitats in cold climates pp42-43, 46-47 migration p53

Antarctica

Antarctica is one and a half times the size of the USA. Nearly all the land is covered with a massive ice cap thousands of metres thick.

It is dark all through the winter and light all through the summer. Lichens and a few types of moss manage to grow on patches of bare rock. There are no large land animals. Most life is in the sea. Shrimps, or krill, feed on algae. Krill and small fish are food for the larger animals – baleen whales, fur seals, seals and penguins.

The animals of the Antarctic are well protected against the cold. The fur seal, which is a type of sea-lion, has a thick coat of soft fur. Seals and penguins have a layer of blubber (fat under their skin). Penguins also have long thin feathers like a tight coat.

Did you know...?

Antarctica's ice cap contains 90% of the world's fresh water. If all the ice melted, the level of the oceans would rise by 65 m.

Millions of years ago, all the continents were joined together.

Antarctica and Australia were joined until about 45 million years ago.

46

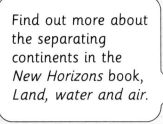

Find out more about the separating continents in the *New Horizons* book, *Land, water and air*.

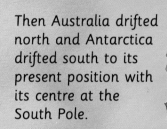

Then Australia drifted north and Antarctica drifted south to its present position with its centre at the South Pole.

The Emperor penguins' year

There are millions of penguins in the waters around Antarctica. The largest are the Emperor penguins. They spend the summer months in the sea, fattening up for the winter. They come ashore in March, ready to mate and lay their eggs. Penguins do not build nests. The female lays one egg. She then goes back to the sea to feed. The male puts the egg on his feet, under a fold of his stomach. He stands like this for two months, keeping the egg warm.

When the chick hatches, the female returns, bringing food. Now the male can go to feed. When he returns with more food for the chick, the parents take it in turns to go fishing until summer arrives.

More about: habitats in cold climates pp42-45 the Poles pp44-45

Australia

Australia is an isolated island – the largest in the world. Animals and plants which evolved in other parts of the world could not easily reach it. So Australia has its own species of animals and plants. Another reason for this is its landscape and climate.

It is the flattest and driest continent in the world. Rain falls on the north and the east coast, but does not spread any further. So most of Australia is desert and scrubland. Eucalyptus and acacia are two plants which manage to grow in this difficult climate. They are very hardy with small evergreen leaves.

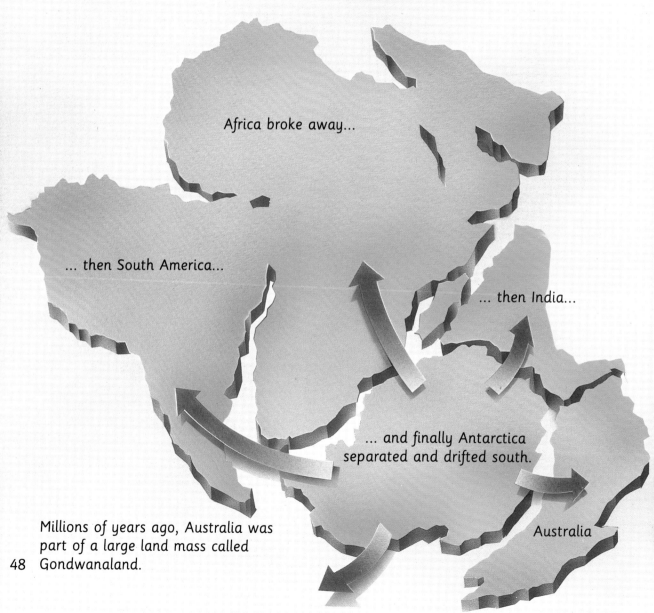

Africa broke away...

... then South America...

... then India...

... and finally Antarctica separated and drifted south.

Australia

Millions of years ago, Australia was part of a large land mass called Gondwanaland.

Australian mammals

Most of the world's mammals are **placental**. Their babies develop in the mother's womb. Placental mammals evolved in Asia and spread to other parts of the world, but they could not reach Australia. The **marsupials**, or pouched animals, such as kangaroos, arrived in Australia much earlier when it was joined to Antarctica and South America. Without competition from the placental mammals, they could develop and thrive. Then settlers brought placental mammals such as rabbits to Australia. These animals began to compete with the marsupials for food and territory.

Find out more about placental and marsupial mammals in the *New Horizons* book, *Life around us.*

Alice Springs is one of the few places in the centre of Australia where there is enough rainfall for plants to grow.

Similar groups

Some marsupial mammals are very similar to placental mammals in other parts of the world. Kangaroos are not like anything else, but there are marsupial wolves, cats, mice, squirrels, anteaters and bears. This is another example of convergent evolution.
Try to find pictures of these, and any other examples.

Did you know...?

Koala bears are the only animals to feed on eucalyptus leaves. They have developed a way to digest the tough, strong-tasting leaves.

49

More about: eucalyptus p40   desert pp30-33   islands pp50-51

Colonising an island

It is easy to see how animals and plants spread across large land masses, but how did they reach remote islands?

The Hawaiian islands

When these volcanic islands were first formed there was no life on them. They are more than 3000 km from North America. Some types of plants and animals have managed to get there, but others have not. There are no reptiles, amphibians, freshwater fish or land mammals on the islands, apart from those brought in by people.

Only a few families of birds, insects and plants reached the Hawaiian islands. This was an advantage for them. There was not nearly as much competition for survival as there was in other parts of the world. The animals and plants could adapt to suit all the habitats.

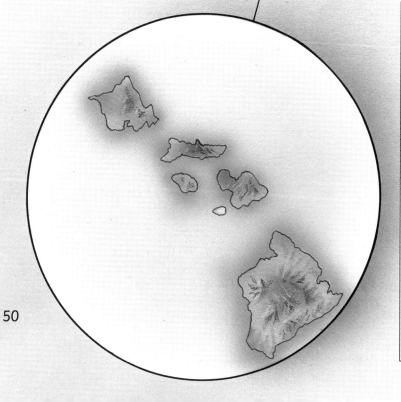

Did you know...?

- Many of the plants and animals on these islands are not found anywhere else in the world – 91% of Hawaiian flowering plants, nearly 99% of Hawaiian birds and 100% of Hawaiian insects are found only in Hawaii.

- One type of tree snail reached Hawaii. From this, at least 189 species have evolved. Each has a different pattern on its shell. Why do you think this is?

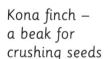

Green honeycreeper

The threat to Hawaiian wildlife

Hawaiian wildlife is now being threatened by people and the animals and plants they have brought to the islands. For example, the plant life is at risk from goats. Some of the birds have already died out. Efforts are now being made to protect the species that live there.

Apapane –
a useful
all-round beak

Iiwi –
a beak for
sipping nectar

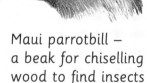

Kona finch –
a beak for
crushing seeds

Maui parrotbill –
a beak for chiselling
wood to find insects

More than 500 types of fruit fly have evolved from one species which arrived in Hawaii millions of years ago. This is a quarter of all the types of fruit fly in the world.

giant fruit fly

A family of finchlike birds arrived on the islands about 15 million years ago. This one species evolved into 40 types of finches called honeycreepers. Some eat insects. Others feed on fruit, seeds, or nectar. The beak of each species has adapted to suit its diet.

How do you think plant seeds reached the Hawaiian islands? How are goats threatening plant life there?

51

More about: beaks p17   endangered species pp58–61

Life in the sea

The oceans cover nearly three-quarters of the Earth. Sea water is full of tiny algae called plankton. Sea animals depend on this for food in the same way that land animals depend on plants.

Plankton-eaters

It is very dark in the depths of the oceans. There is no plankton here. Plankton-eaters have to swim nearer the surface to feed. When they return to the depths, they become food for the predators that live near the sea bed.

Some of the giants of the sea, such as the basking shark and the whale shark, feed on plankton.

Algae plankton need sunlight, water and carbon dioxide to make their own food. They do this in the same way as plants on land.

Minute animal plankton feed on the algae.

Small fish such as herrings, anchovies and shrimps feed on plankton.

Larger fish such as sharks feed on the smaller ones.

The manta ray has a huge mouth for gulping sea water. Slits in the side of its head allow the water to flow out again. The plankton are removed by a 'sieving' action inside the mouth of the fish.

Did you know...?
One cubic metre of water might contain 200 000 plankton.

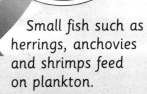

Migration in the sea

Some sea animals migrate to different areas to mate and bear their young, or to find more food. Humpback whales spend the summer in the cold polar waters, feeding on krill (shrimps). When winter arrives, they swim towards warmer waters near the equator to have their babies. Grey whales swim nearly 10 000 km from the Arctic to the Pacific coast of Mexico to bear their young.

Environments in the sea

The different environments in the sea can be compared with the environments on land. Each one has its own animals which have adapted to suit the habitat.

On a coral reef

Coral is the outer skeleton of a soft-bodied animal called a coral polyp. The skeletons build up to form a huge reef with branches like trees. Brightly-coloured fish swim about among the branches. There are lobsters, sea urchins and snails with colourful patterned shells. Sponges and seaweeds grow on the reef. Sometimes a shark swims in to prowl for food.

The open sea, where large shoals of fish graze on plankton, is the savanna.

Near the edges of the continents, the sea bed is sandy and there is not much food for the few animals which live there. These areas are the deserts of the sea.

Coral reefs, with their large variety of brightly-coloured fish and invertebrates, are the tropical rain forests of the sea.

53

More about: desert pp30-33   migration p45   the Poles pp44-47

In the dark

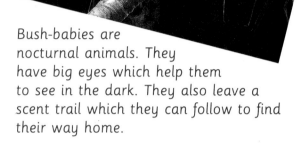

Some animals make their homes underground. Rabbits, badgers, mongooses and prairie dogs use their homes to hide from predators and to sleep in. They come out to find food.

Desert animals live underground to escape from the heat of the day and the cold of the night, as well as from predators. Badgers hibernate in their burrows in winter.

Some animals which live underground are nocturnal and others come out during the day. Some never come out at all.

Bush-babies are nocturnal animals. They have big eyes which help them to see in the dark. They also leave a scent trail which they can follow to find their way home.

Prairie dogs spend daylight hours on the surface and sleep in the burrows at night.

A prairie dog town

Prairie dogs live on the prairies of North America.

The 'house' has a main entrance at the surface.

Each family lives in a series of burrows linked by passages, like rooms in a house. The family consists of one male and several females with their young. Each female has her own burrow.

Did you know...?

Some prairie dog towns grow very big. One in Texas covered an area 380 km long and 160 km wide. It was home to about 400 million prairie dogs.

Other families build similar burrow systems nearby. Two or more of these make up a town.

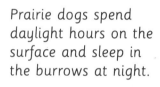

The naked mole rat

These strange creatures live in Kenya in Africa. They are never seen above ground, but spend their lives in long underground tunnels. The land is dry for most of the year and many of the plants store water in underground **tubers**. The mole rats feed on these tubers.

Mole rats work in communities. The young ones, which are about 7 cm long, work in a long line, digging new tunnels. As they grow bigger, they do less work. The biggest are the warriors.

The naked mole rat has no fur. Its skin is pink and wrinkled and its eyes are tiny.

They spend most of their time sleeping in the nest chamber, but if a predator manages to get into the tunnels, they rush to attack it.

Moles

Moles spend most of their lives underground. Molehills on the surface are the only sign that they are around. Moles have a good sense of smell which helps them to find food, but they are almost blind.

Find out more about nocturnal animals in the *New Horizons* book, *Life around us.*

Moles dig or 'paddle' through the soil with strong front feet, searching for earthworms and insect grubs.

55

More about: desert pp30-33   nocturnal animals pp18, 25

The effect of people

Animals and plants have always had to compete for survival. But now, the biggest threat to most of them is people.

People live in many regions of the world. The first people were hunters and gatherers. They spread all over the world and adapted to the different climates. As soon as groups of people began to settle in one place, they cleared land to grow crops and to build towns and cities. Over the years, they have destroyed many wildlife habitats.

Today, the world is very crowded. People have powerful machines. They can chop down forests very quickly and plough up huge areas of land for new buildings.

Living together

There is now less open countryside, so it is harder for some wildlife to survive. But some wild animals have adapted. Jackdaws, rooks and starlings nest in city centres. What other examples of urban wildlife can you think of?

The spreading desert

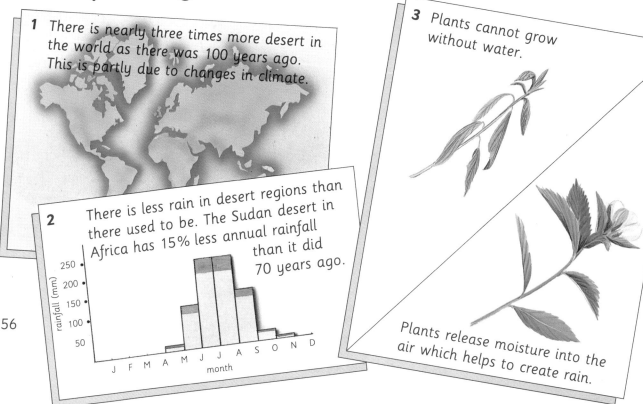

1 There is nearly three times more desert in the world as there was 100 years ago. This is partly due to changes in climate.

2 There is less rain in desert regions than there used to be. The Sudan desert in Africa has 15% less annual rainfall than it did 70 years ago.

3 Plants cannot grow without water.

Plants release moisture into the air which helps to create rain.

People's effect on people

When people first settled down in groups, some became more powerful than others. There were battles for land.

When people conquer lands or settle in a new place, they may try to change the people who already live there. Sometimes, they destroy their customs and way of life.

Some of the Indians who live in the Amazon rain forest are hunters and gatherers. Chopping down the forests forces them to change the way they have always lived.

Find out more about rainfall in the *New Horizons* book, *Land, water and air.*

Did you know...?

Many scientists think that 'modern' humans evolved in Africa and began to spread across the world about 100 000 years ago.

4 As the plants disappear, the climate becomes drier and drier.

5 Over-grazing by animals is also contributing to the problem.

Nomads move around in desert areas, looking for grazing land.

6 Their animals eat the meagre grass, then the shrubs. The plants disappear and new ones may not grow.

Eventually, semi-desert areas become true desert.

57

More about: rain forest pp38-39 grasslands pp20-21, 26-27, 34-37

Animals in danger

When a habitat is destroyed, some animals manage to adapt to a new environment. Others die out.

People need land and they need wood. The rain forests are the only very large forests left, and now they are being chopped down. Large animals such as the tiger and the orang-utan are dying out because their habitats are disappearing.

The snow leopard (above), tiger and Asiatic cheetah are in danger of becoming extinct, because they have been killed for their fur.

QUAGGA MALE

People have always hunted animals. At first, they killed them for food. Then they began to hunt for sport as well. European settlers in South Africa found huge herds of antelope and a type of zebra called the quagga (above). They hunted these animals until there were hardly any antelope and the quagga had died out completely.

Rhinoceroses are hunted for their horns (right), elephants for their ivory tusks and whales for their oil. All these animals could soon become extinct.

Large animals are in the greatest danger. One reason is because they are easiest for hunters to spot. Can you think of any other reasons?

58

Barn owls in danger

In Britain, barn owls have almost disappeared because:

- they have lost their habitat;
- they have been poisoned by chemicals in the food chain.

When farmers use chemicals to keep pests off their crops

How the food chain should work

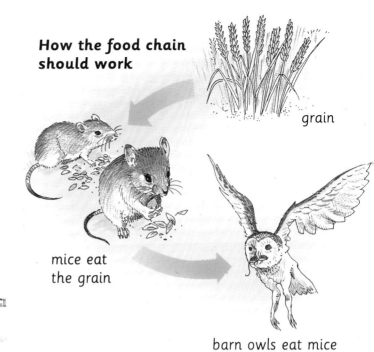

grain

mice eat the grain

barn owls eat mice

chemicals poison mice; they die

barn owls die out; they are poisoned by the chemicals eaten by mice

Earlier harvesting

harvest mice are forced out of the fields where they used to nest

no large families of mice

barn owls die out; there is no prey to hunt

Did you know...?

About 60 000 plants may become extinct during the next 50 years. If people carry on chopping down the rain forests, several hundred types of animal and more than a million types of insect will die out.

59

More about: extinction pp56-57, 60-61 food chain pp14-15, 52

Protecting wildlife

Many people are worried about the dangers to wildlife. They try to protect it. **Ecologists** are people who study how animals and plants live together. They are worried about the way habitats are being destroyed. In many parts of the world, there is no longer room for large animals to roam in the wild.

Nature reserves

One way to protect animals and plants is to create a habitat for them by dedicating land as nature reserves.

It is difficult to set aside nature reserves in countries like Britain which are already crowded with people and their buildings. Even so, there are some areas, like Cwm Idwal in Snowdonia, where wildlife is protected. People are not allowed to build on or change this land in any way.

In areas like the Amazon rain forests in South America, there is still room to create large protected reserves. In parts of East Africa, animals roam wild on grassland game reserves.

Groups such as Greenpeace fight against hunting and poaching of wild animals. Here, they are in action against a Japanese whaling catcher ship in the Southern Ocean.

About six out of every hundred plant species are in danger of dying out because of building towns and roads, farming, fumes from traffic, chemical weed and pest killers, and over-collection by people.

Yellowstone National Park in the USA is home to elk (above), grizzly bears, wolves and mountain lions.

Protecting species

Zoos and wildlife parks also protect animals, though not always in surroundings as natural as in the wild. But animals are safe from hunters and pairs might breed.

Plants can be protected by trying to prevent people from digging them up, cutting down hedgerows and using chemicals on land. In some cases, places where rare or endangered plants grow are a closely-guarded secret.

Is there a nature reserve near you? Nature reserves display a lot of information about the species of animals and plants you might see. If you can visit one, find out about the types of wildlife that live there. What does this tell you about the habitat?

Films and videos are a useful way of showing people different habitats around the world and the danger that wildlife is in.

61

More about: endangered species pp56-59 loss of habitat pp51, 56-59

Key words

The meanings of words can depend on how and when they are used. You may find that as you learn more about science the meanings change slightly.

acidic soil soil which contains very little lime. Rain washes away lime and other minerals and makes the soil sour. A few plants can grow only in acidic soil, but most need neutral or alkaline soil

adapted changed to suit different surroundings

alkaline soil soil which contains a lot of lime

camouflage colourings or markings which help animals hide against their background

canopy the highest layer of branches in a forest

carnivores animals which feed on meat (other animals)

climate the usual weather conditions of an area or country

colonise to take root or make a home in a new place

coniferous this describes a tree such as a pine or a fir, which has needles instead of leaves and produces seeds in a cone

convergent evolution the term used when animals living in different parts of the world evolve in the same way

deciduous this describes a tree which loses its leaves in winter

domestic this describes a wild animal which has been tamed

drought dryness, no rain

ecologist someone who studies the way plants and animals live together and affect each other

environment surroundings

evolution the process of changing and adapting to suit the surroundings

extinct an animal or plant that has died out

hardy able to live in cold conditions and frosty weather

herbivores animals which feed on plants

hostile difficult or harsh

humid moist, damp

invertebrates animals which do not have a backbone

marsupial a mammal which carries its developing baby in a pouch

monsoon strong wind bringing heavy rain to South East Asia in summer

nocturnal nocturnal animals are awake at night and sleep in the daytime

neutral soil soil which is not acidic or alkaline

nomads animals or people who move around in search of food

nutrients substances which provide food for a living thing

permafrost the layer of frozen soil beneath the surface in the tundra

placental mammals whose babies develop in the mother's womb. The placenta is an organ in the mother's womb which allows food and oxygen to reach the baby and takes harmful waste away

predators animals which hunt other animals for food

prey the animals hunted by predators

reach an area of a river

scarce hard to find

species a group of animals or plants which are all the same or very similar to one another

temperate a climate which has warm summers and cool winters

temperature the amount of heat in something, measured with a thermometer

thrive to grow healthily

tropical the climate near the equator

tuber the swollen underground root of some plants: a potato is a tuber

venomous a venomous animal can poison other animals, usually by biting or stinging

Index